TABLE OF CONTENTS

Kevin Garnett scores two points for the Celtics during Game 6.

WINNING IT ALL

Boston Celtics' head coach Doc Rivers called for a **time-out**. His team was losing to the Los Angeles Lakers. They were playing Game 6 of the 2008 National Basketball Association (NBA) **Finals**. Boston had already won three games in the series. If they could win Game 6, they would be the NBA champions.

Boston **forward** Kevin Garnett knew that his team would have to play better **defense** to win the game. "The defense is our backbone," said Kevin. He and his teammates were up to the challenge. Kevin jumped to grab **rebounds**. He soared through the air to **block** shots.

The Celtics' efforts paid off. By **halftime**, Boston had the lead, 58–35. Lakers' star Kobe Bryant knew that his team was in for a fight. "They were definitely the best defense I've seen the entire **playoffs**," Kobe said.

Kevin plays tough defense against the Lakers' Pau Gasol during the first quarter of Game 6.

Kevin and the Celtics didn't slow down in the second half. Boston player Paul Pierce made shot after shot. Kevin grabbed more rebounds. The crowd roared around him. Boston won the game, 131–92. The Celtics were NBA champions!

With this victory, the Celtics had won the NBA championship for the 17th time. This is more than any other team in NBA history. But 2008 marked the first championship for Kevin and his teammates.

Paul Pierce *(center)* shoots over Lakers' players Ronny Turiaf *(left)* and Kobe Bryant *(right)*.